9317

92
Truman   Miklowitz, Gloria D.
H.   Harry Truman / by Gloria Miklowitz ;
           illustrated by Janet Scabrini. New York
           : G. P. Putnam's Sons, c1975.
             62 p. : ill. ; 23 cm. (A See and read
           book)
             A biography of the "common man" from
           Missouri who became the thirty-third
           President of the United States.

             1. Truman, Harry S., Pres., U.S.,
           1884-1972. 2. Presidents.
           I. Scabrini, Janet. II. Title

       31 MAR 77   1976600   ICRNcs   74-83008

About The Book

Harry Truman was a happy, curious boy, even though he had some difficulties as a boy. By the time he was six, his family had moved three times and it was not always easy to make friends. His poor eyesight meant that he couldn't join in the rough and tumble games with other boys, so he was by himself a lot, until he reached high school. He loved to read, especially history, and he took piano lessons. The other children teased him about his lessons, but Harry didn't care.

As a young man, Harry Truman served in World War I and was a popular leader among his men. He returned to Independence, Missouri, and entered public life as a judge. But he never envisioned that he would become the thirty-third President of the United States. He is remembered for his honesty, directness, and plain-speaking ways.

Harry Truman

by Gloria Miklowitz

illustrated by Janet Scabrini

G. P. Putnam's Sons   New York

Acknowledgment

The author would like to express her gratitude for the encouragement and help given by Dr. Edward Pfeiffer, researcher at the Harry S. Truman Library, Independence, Missouri.

9 3 1 7

Text copyright © 1975 by Gloria D. Miklowitz
Illustrations copyright © 1975 by Janet Scabrini
All rights reserved. Published simultaneously in
Canada by Longman Canada Limited, Toronto.
SBN: GB-399-60918-0
SBN: TR-399-20427-x
Library of Congress Catalog Card Number: 74-83008
PRINTED IN THE UNITED STATES OF AMERICA
07209

"What are we going to do?"
Martha Truman asked her husband
when their first child was born.
"Your father wants him named
Solomon, after him. My father
wants him named Anderson Shippe,
after him. And I want him named
Harrison, after my brother!"

John Truman stood by his wife's bed in the six-foot-wide bedroom of their small farmhouse. It was May 8, 1884, in Lamar, Missouri. Outside, Mr. Truman could see the young pine tree he had just planted in honor of his little son. Beyond the tree was the large barn where he kept the mules he sold for a living.

"We'll call him Harry then. Harry S. Truman. The S can be for both your father and mine."

"I like that!" Martha Truman said, smiling. "Harry S. Truman. Yes, that will do very nicely."

By the time Harry was six his
father had moved three times.
He had done poorly as a mule trader and
farmer, so he moved to Independence,
Missouri, hoping to do better
in a bigger town. While Harry,
his brother and sister were growing
up, John Truman did well in real
estate and farming.

Before he was six, Harry had many accidents. He broke his collarbone, nearly choked on a peach pit, and almost lost a toe. Then, just before he was to start school, his mother found that he could hardly see.

She took him to an eye doctor. "He's as blind as a mole," the doctor said. "He'll have to wear very thick glasses. And, Harry," the doctor went on, "you'll have to be careful. No more hard play. You might break your glasses."

As if this weren't bad enough, in second grade Harry caught a sickness called diphtheria. For months he couldn't move his arms or legs. He was nine years old, but his mother had to wheel him in a baby carriage to give him fresh air.

Because of Harry's physical problems, he spent a lot of time alone. At ten, he started to study the piano. He would wake at 5 A.M. each day to practice for two hours before going to school. "Sissy! Sissy!" some boys called him, but Harry ignored them.

When Harry was only four, his mother had taught him to read. He loved to read. His favorite books were *Heroes of History,* about famous men and women. By the time he was twelve he had read the Bible twice and most of the 3,500 books in the local library.

Harry's teen years were happy ones. He belonged to the "Waldo Street Gang." The group of boys and girls did everything together. They swam in the local pond in

summer, skated on its ice in winter,
and played baseball and other games.

Bess Wallace was one of the
gang. He had met her in Sunday
school and fallen in love instantly.
She was a pretty blue-eyed blond
tomboy. She could "whistle through
her teeth" and was very good at
baseball.

Although he worked at a drugstore every day, Harry did well in high school. History and Latin were his best subjects. His closest friend was Charlie Ross, son of the town jailer. They sometimes cut school together. Later, Charlie became a top newsman and President Truman's press secretary.

When Harry was graduated from high school in 1901, his English teacher, Miss Tillie Brown, kissed Charlie Ross, her best pupil.

"How about a kiss for me?" Harry asked.

"Not until you've done something to deserve it," Miss Tillie said.

Years later Harry called his old teacher from Washington. "Miss Brown, this is the President of the United States. Do I get that kiss now?"

Harry wanted to go to college very badly, but his father lost all his money at this time. "If I can get into West Point or Annapolis," he told his parents, "I could get a fine education, free."

He started studying for the Army and Navy school tests. But one day he visited an Army recruiting station. "Sorry, son. Your eyes are too bad, no matter what grades you make," he was told.

His family needed money, so
Harry went to work. For $35 a
month he worked as timekeeper for
the railroad. Then he worked in a
mailroom. Next, he worked as a
bank clerk, a very dull job, and as a
bookkeeper. During these years he
also joined the National Guard.

In 1906 Harry's father asked him
to take care of the 600-acre family
farm. For the next eight years
Harry did everything there was to
do on a farm. He also found time
to see Bess Wallace.

When the United States entered
World War I, Harry's National
Guard unit was sworn into the
Army. Harry was asked to start an
Army store at first. In six months
he had the store working so well
that it made $15,000. Then he was
made captain of an Army unit. The
men in his unit were known to be
very hard to work with, but Harry
won them over. His men would do
anything for him. Together, they
fought in France until the war ended.

On June 28, 1919, Major Harry
S. Truman married Bess Wallace.
Soon after he opened a men's
clothing store with an Army friend.
The store did well at first. His
Army buddies came in to talk, as
well as to buy. Harry's fairness and

good sense made everyone like
him. But in 1922, when business
was bad all over the country,
Harry's store failed. He owed
people a great deal of money. It
took years, but he paid back every
penny.

One of Harry's Army friends
was Jim Pendergast. Jim's father Mike,
and uncle Tom, led the state's
Democratic Party. If they said,
"Vote for this man," Democrats all over
Missouri listened.

Jim told his father how much
Harry knew about history and
current events and how well liked
he was. Mike Pendergast asked if
Harry would like to run for judge of
Jackson County.

When Harry said yes, Mike
Pendergast called his Democratic club
together. "Now I'm going to tell
you who you'll support for county
judge," he said. "It's Harry Truman.
He's a returned soldier, a captain
with a fine record, and his men
loved him."

Harry won his first election by
less than 500 votes. From 1922 to
1924 he served as judge while
going to law school at night. But
the most important thing that
happened in those years was the
birth of his daughter, Mary Margaret
Truman, he said years later.

Without a job in 1925, Harry
sold automobile club memberships
for a while, but he was not happy.
He had loved working for the
people, in government. He decided

to go see Tom Pendergast. "I want
to get back into politics," he said. Tom
helped Harry get elected again.

In his new job as presiding judge,
Harry "fired people right and left
who didn't work in the county's
interest." He was very unpopular
with dishonest people.

31

Harry wanted better roads, a new hospital, and a courthouse in the county. "No one's going to vote money for that!" everyone said. Harry didn't agree.

He went to all the small towns and farms in the county and told people about the need for better roads. When election time came, the people voted the money for his plan.

In 1934 Harry was fifty years old. He still wanted to serve his country. Tom Pendergast offered him the chance. "I'd like you to run for the United States Senate," he said.

Harry thought fast. He knew he wasn't the first choice. He knew people might think he'd take his orders from Pendergast if he won.

"I have no money," he said quietly. "And I'm not very well known. But I'll try my darndest!"

He *did* try his darndest. A man can do anything he sets his mind to, Harry believed. Sometimes he made fifteen to twenty speeches a day. He talked to people anyplace he could find them—in grocery stores, on the street, at barbershops. He'd say, "I was a farmer and a failed businessman, and I understand your problems, because I'm just like you."

He told them Franklin Roosevelt was a good President because he really cared about helping the people. People liked the way Harry said exactly what was on his mind. They elected him Senator.

In January, 1935, he went to Washington. He was not a college graduate, had no money, and was still "the farm boy from Missouri" to many people. But he made many friends. People couldn't help liking this friendly, hardworking, and honest man.

In Washington he worked long days, starting at five thirty each morning. In the evening he would go home for dinner with Bess and Margaret. He would play the piano or listen to Margaret sing.

Late in the evening, he would turn to the many papers he brought home. He always wanted to understand everything about the problems he might have to vote on. Once, he read fifty books about the railroad so he could make wise decisions on railroad problems.

World War II had started in
Europe when he was reelected to
the Senate in 1940. America was
busy building factories to make
guns and planes. Senator Truman
was amazed at the waste he saw.
He wanted to look into how
government money was being
spent. With only $15,000 to work
with, the Truman Committee visited
shipyards, mines, and factories.
It reported dishonesty and told of
ways to save money and stop
waste. Because of its work, the
government saved $200,000,000.

On December 7, 1941, Japan bombed Pearl Harbor in Hawaii. America was now at war. During the next years, the Truman Commitee saved the country $10 billion. Once it forced an aircraft company to remake more than 400 badly made engines so pilots would not be killed.

People who had never liked Truman now spoke well of him. Newsmen voted him the man, next to the President, who had done most for the war effort.

When President Franklin D.
Roosevelt was elected for the
fourth time, Harry S. Truman
became his Vice President.
Roosevelt was very sick, but he
was in the middle of a war. He had
to go on.

On April 12, 1944, Truman had been Vice President for only eighty-two days. He was at an evening meeting when he got a phone call from Roosevelt's press secretary. "Please come right over," he said in a tight voice.

Truman got his hat, raced out of the building, and ordered his car. He rushed to Mrs. Roosevelt's study at the White House.

"Harry," Mrs. Roosevelt said, "the President is dead."

"Is there anything I can do for you?" Truman asked, tears running down his cheeks.

Knowing Truman would now take over as President, Mrs. Roosevelt put out a comforting hand. "Is there any way we can help *you*?" she asked.

At 7:09 P.M. Harry S. Truman was sworn in as the thirty-third President of the United States.

There was so much to learn. Truman met all day with government and military leaders. Each night he read mountains of reports. He had so much to know and decide about matters at home and in the world.

In July, at a meeting with two other world leaders, Truman learned that an atomic bomb had been tested in New Mexico and it worked.

Most of the men who had worked on the bomb told him to use it if Japan wouldn't give up. "I wanted to save a half million boys on our side from being killed, and as many on the other side," the President said. When Japan refused to surrender, Truman ordered that the bomb be dropped, first on Hiroshima, then on Nagasaki. Soon after, Japan surrendered.

When the war was over, Truman turned to problems at home. He asked Congress to pass laws to help people get better houses and jobs, health care, education, old age benefits and equal rights. Congress refused.

Today Americans of different colors and sex have equal rights *by law*. Old people have better health care and other help because of new laws. These are the kinds of laws Truman wanted twenty-five years ago.

Although Congress wouldn't pass the laws he wanted at home, it passed laws he wanted to help Europe rebuild after the war. The U.S. sent help to countries trying to stay free. "I believe we must help free peoples to work out their own future in their own way," Truman said. He made many friends for the United States in the world. He backed the idea of Israel becoming a nation.

It was hard work being President. There was little time for playing the piano, listening to Margaret sing, or reading just for fun. The President worked sixteen to eighteen hours a day. His days were full signing papers, as many as 600 in a day, reading reports, and meeting people.

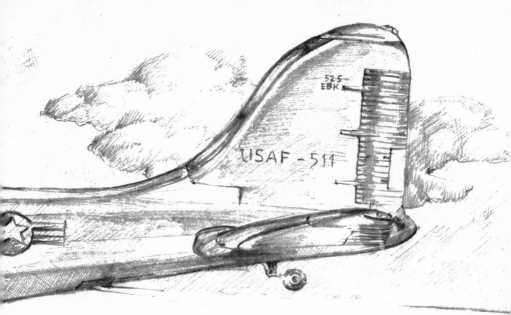

At the end of World War II, the
Soviet Union occupied a part of
Germany. Just before the 1948
election, the Soviet Union closed
off the city of Berlin in Germany so
no food or supplies could come in.
It was a first step in trying to make
Germany a Communist country.
Some people wanted to go to war
with the Soviet Union over this.
Truman said, "There will be no
shooting."

Instead, he ordered an airlift.
American planes flew supplies into
Berlin until the Soviet Union
opened the city again.

It seemed impossible for Truman
to be reelected. Running against
him was the well-to-do, well-liked
governor of New York, Thomas E.
Dewey. Eight out of ten newspapers
said Dewey would win.

From September until the
election in November Truman
traveled by train to speak directly
to the American people. Thousands
turned out to hear him. They loved
it when he introduced Bess and
Margaret as "the boss" and "my
baby, the boss's boss."

He was a man of the people
—hardworking and honest. He
wanted people to have better lives
and they knew it. He beat Dewey
by 2,000,000 votes.

The Trumans lived next door to
the White House while the White
House was being repaired. One day
two men tried to kill the President.
They suddenly started shooting at
the house. In three minutes,
thirty-one shots were fired.

"A President has to expect those things," Truman said. He kept all his appointments that day as if nothing had happened.

Congress still would not pass laws Truman asked for to give a "fair deal" to the people. But Congress did pass laws to help arm America's friends. Truman believed that if America's friends were strong, America would be strong, too.

When the country of North Korea invaded South Korea in June, 1950, Truman sent American troops in to help. It was four years before the North Koreans agreed to peace terms.

Truman left the White House in 1953 to return to his home in Independence. People loved to stand outside his home to watch for Bess and him. At home, the former President kept busy writing books and planning for the building of the Truman Library and Museum, which opened in 1957 in Independence, Missouri.

To the very last days of his life, Harry S. Truman was a fighter. Doctors said he couldn't live, yet he held on day after day, proving them wrong.

Harry S. Truman—farmer, soldier, judge, Senator, Vice President, President, and man of the people—died at the age of eighty-eight on December 26, 1972.

The Author

Gloria Miklowitz was born in New York City and received her BS degree from the University of Michigan at Ann Arbor. She wrote documentary films for five years for the U.S. Naval Undersea Research and Development Center and then started writing for children. She is married to Professor Julius Miklowitz of the California Institute of Technology, and they have two sons.

The Artist

Janet Scabrini was born in Buffalo, New York, where she spent her childhood.

At the moment she is a last-year art student at the Pratt Institute in New York. When she is not involved in her art, she works in photography. This is her first book.